# *How to Play*

# CHAMPIONSHIP

# BASEBALL

# OSCAR FRALEY

*How to Play*

## CHAMPIONSHIP
## BASEBALL

*Pictures by* CHARLES YERKOW

A. A. WYN, INC., NEW YORK

To my son

**MIKE**

*With high hopes for him and all the
other Little Leaguers of today who
will be the Big Leaguers of tomorrow.*

# Contents

# Introduction

If you have baseball ambitions, you can be a major league star!

The formula is simple. Pick a position for which you have the necessary physical assets explained in this volume and then learn to play that position skillfully.

Actually there is no physical pattern demanded to attain success in the game of baseball. The pictures of the great Major Leaguers represented in this book will prove this to you.

Being small of stature is no impossible handicap. Proof of this is verified in such brilliant big league stars as Phil Rizzuto, Peewee Reese and Harry Brecheen, who contribute in this book secrets which carried them to the heights.

Rizzuto is only five feet, six inches tall and weighs 155 pounds but when he hangs up his glove, there will be a place waiting for him in baseball's Hall of Fame. Reese, like Brecheen, is five feet, nine inches tall. Yet the little Colonel from Louisville ranks with the great shortstops of all time while Brecheen proves that it is not necessary to be a physical giant to hurl your way into the record books.

Branch Rickey, the shrewd baseball man who laid the foundation for great Dodger teams, always claimed that he wanted his ballplayers to be fast of foot, have a strong arm and be able to hit. Yet it was Rickey who said of little Eddie Stanky:

"He can't run, can't throw and can't hit—but he's one of the finest baseball players I ever saw."

Clint Courtney, who will show you tricks in handling the mask and mitt, is only five feet, eight inches and weighs a bulky 180 pounds. He can't run like a deer and he won't break down many fences with his bat, but he is one of the finest catchers in the big leagues.

The reason for his success is obvious. He has a burning desire to play baseball—and to play it right.

Every spring when the big league clubs take their crop of rookies to training camp, harried coaches must spend long, tedious hours correcting faults developed on the sandlots or in the minors. They may be small faults, but they spell the difference between making the big league grade and returning to the "bushes." Through the years those little flaws have unfortunately become an ingrained part of the player's automatic actions, no matter how hard the coaches struggle to correct them. This is the main factor in keeping so many promising young players out of the big leagues.

The full step-by-step picture story of the big league way has never been presented before, and so this book is designed to give you that story in more than 400 pictures which reveal tricks of the trade at every position.

Special thanks are due to the great players who took time out during a hot pennant race to pose, and who provide the tips which will help hopeful youngsters fill their shoes in the future. In his eagerness to help the kids coming up, each reveals that he is a champion in more ways than one.

Through the faithful eye of the lightning-fast sequence camera, you can learn the complete story of how these Big Leaguers carry out their assignments in the letter-perfect fashion demanded under baseball's big top. Because the sequence camera freezes the action completely at every important phase of the game, whether it is pitching, hitting or fielding, the machine-like play which can be your pattern to success is clearly revealed.

Absorb it, put it into action—and you're on your way!

OSCAR FRALEY,
Huntington, L. I.

# How to Play

# CHAMPIONSHIP

# BASEBALL

# 1. Fast Ball Pitching

## As demonstrated by
## ALLIE REYNOLDS
### New York Yankees

The payoff pitch of big league baseball is the fast ball, demonstrated here by Allie Reynolds of the New York Yankees who has one of the best of all time.

From the days of Walter Johnson, on down through Dizzy Dean and Bob Feller, the highest salaried hurlers were the ones with the blinding speed. It was the big pitch for Reynolds as he led the Yankees to pennant after pennant.

It is a delivery which requires a strong arm and fine control, for inability to put it over the plate makes it virtually worthless. Also it is a pitch which must have "something on it" because, as Joe DiMaggio once said: "They'll hit it if it's shot out of a cannon unless the ball is working."

This doesn't mean that the fast ball must do the tricks of a curve or a knuckle ball. As a matter of fact, the break of a fast ball may hardly be noticeable. But it must be there. The speed and manner of delivery will put that "work" on the ball.

Reynolds, as you will note in the accompanying sequence pictures, uses an almost full overhand delivery. This means that his fast ball rises slightly as it nears the plate.

Virtually the same action occurs from a three-quarter overhand delivery, although the ball might have a tendency to break back toward the same side from which it was thrown. On a side-arm delivery, the ball would break back toward that same side.

Due to the fact that the overhand delivery rises, players with this delivery are inclined to be high ball pitchers. To bring the ball down in the strike zone, the ball must be held a trifle longer.

As for the grip on the ball, you will see in Reynolds' various grips that he holds every pitch in the same manner, with the index and middle fingers together and the third and little fingers folded under.

"You hold them all the same so that the hitter never can tell from your grip what you are going to throw," Allie explains. "It's all in the way you let the ball go as to just what type of a pitch you make. For instance, I let my fast ball go with the index and middle fingers straight over the top, keeping a tight grip until it spins out of my fingers."

To throw his change up, or slow ball, Reynolds simply takes a looser grip on the ball, as you will note in the respective finger

## REYNOLDS PITCHING THE
## FAST BALL

1

2

3

4

5

6

7

8

9

10

11

12

13

14

15

## CLOSE-UP OF REYNOLDS' DELIVERY

1

2

3

4

5

6

7

**8**

**9**

**10**

**11**

**12**

**13**

**14**

**15**

**Reynolds' pitching position**

**Letting go of the fast pitch**

**Allie's tight grip for a fast ball**

where the stitches are close together. Others like to get those two close rows of stitches running across their fingers. For those with large hands, as in Reynolds' case, it doesn't make much difference how it is held.

Generally speaking, in making the pitch, the arm, leg and body action should be the same for all types of deliveries so that the batter will not know what is coming. However, a variation may be made occasionally in the number of preliminary arm windups as this confuses the hitter and possibly affects his timing. One of the cagiest pitchers in the matter of confusing batters with various types of windups was Satchel Paige.

Nevertheless, worrying too much about the windup and trying to "trick it up" may do more harm than good, as an excess would tire the pitcher and cause him to lose his control and effectiveness. The main thing to remember in preparing to deliver the ball is to do it comfortably and naturally although, of course, a full windup is inadvisable with men on base.

The sequence pictures of Reynolds' delivery shows why the Yankee siege gun always is so effective. His delivery is so quick and efficient that not many base runners can afford to take liberties with it.

The accompanying picture of Allie's stance

pressure in the grip photographs. It makes no difference to the Super Chief of the Yankees how the ball itself is gripped.

Some pitchers, to obtain a more comfortable grip on the ball and make it "work" for them, put their fingers along the seams

**Reynolds' loose grip for a change
of pace**

**Releasing the curve ball**

with men on base discloses his complete balance.

"This way," he says, "I can hold the runners on and still get all my power into the pitch. But the really important thing is to be completely comfortable, and so the pitcher should take any stance which feels right."

In the full body sequence pictures of Reynolds' throwing his famed fast ball, notice how he rocks back on his left foot as he starts his motion by swinging both arms to the rear, gracefully shifting most of his weight to that rear foot.

His weight still is on the rear foot as the arms swing up and then, as the pitching arm passes over the head and is drawn on back, the body pivots into a tight coil and the weight shifts smoothly to the right leg, with the foot starting its push against the rubber, as the left leg begins the long, balancing stride toward the plate.

When the pitching arm is fully cocked, and the body reared back, the opposite leg is extended fully and still not in contact with the ground. The height of this kick depends on the individual pitcher, although, as you can notice in Reynolds' delivery, the closer it is kept to the ground the quicker the pitch will be gotten off—and the less liberties will

be taken by base runners.

Then, as the pitching arm starts the delivery, the advance foot begins to take the weight of the body—but the rear foot pushes against the rubber until the ball is released.

Note, particularly, at this point, the terrific wrist snap which Reynolds imparts to his pitch.

Also note the slight hop, after the ball is released, with which Allie brings his rear foot forward even with his front foot so that he is in perfect balance to field any ball hit back into his position.

Reynolds, who performed the rare feat of hurling two no-hit, no-run games in 1951, discloses his compact pitching form in the split-second closeup pictures of his "change-up" delivery.

There is a windup variation as he lifts his hands in front of him before swinging them both down and back and then bringing them up for his full windup. For this slow pitch, he loosens his grip on the ball and also imparts much less wrist snap. Actually, all any pitcher does is "take off" the speed of his fast one in delivering a slow ball, although, of course, there are other "slow" pitches.

One of these is the curve ball which, after being perfected, can be delivered either fast or slow. There are many starring pitchers, whose principal weapons consist of a fast ball, change-up and curve. Mixing these up with various speeds—and with control—have enabled them to confound the batters.

Note how similar Reynolds' curve ball is to his fast ball in the pictures of his various grips. The difference is in how he lets go of the ball. His curve ball grip shows how it looks to the batter just before Reynolds snaps the hand over as he releases the ball.

"Just as I let go of the ball, I release the pressure of my index finger and let the ball roll off my middle finger," Allie explains.

So rear back and fire it. The fast ball, and the fast curve, are baseball's big money mixture.

# 2. Curve Ball Pitching

## As demonstrated by
## HARRY BRECHEEN
### Baltimore Orioles

You don't have to be big in stature or have an overpowering fast ball to be a major league pitching star. Proof of that, among others, is little Harry (The Cat) Brecheen who here demonstrates the game's great leveler—the curve ball.

There are some who insist that a baseball doesn't curve. The Boston Red Sox will laugh in their faces. For "The Cat" showed the Red Sox a curve which seemed to come in from first base when the mighty left-hander beat them three times in the 1946 World Series to win the classic almost single-handed for the St. Louis Cardinals.

"The Cat" is a past master with the curve ball, which requires a great amount of practice to perfect. The secret is in releasing the ball with as little effort as possible, perfecting a technique which will not strain the arm, shoulder or wrist as well as evolving a pitch which can be controlled.

Brecheen does, of course, have a fast ball. But his chief stock in trade is that big hook which had the Red Sox' left-handed hitters dropping into the dirt as it jug-handled in over the plate. The beauty of his repertoire was that—as in the case of Reynolds—he held the ball the same way for both pitches and only altered the last part of his delivery, when it was too late to be of any help to the batter.

For the curve starts out much in the same manner of delivery as the fast ball. There is a change only when the elbow of the pitching arm, as it begins to deliver the ball, comes up even with the body.

At that moment the wrist is snapped outward—much as if the hand gave a quick twist while screwing in a light bulb. This causes the ball to break down and to the opposite side from which it was thrown.

As the wrist snaps, the ball is released from between the thumb and index or forefinger. The spin is put on the ball by the wrist action and the second finger.

The grip depends on the individual pitcher. Some like to hold the ball firmly while others prefer a loose grip. Only practice will tell you which method to adopt and how much allowance to make for the "break" of your particular pitch.

In the pictures of Brecheen's grips, note that he holds his fast ball much the same as Reynolds. One of them shows how, in throw-

## THE CURVE BALL, AS PITCHED BY HARRY BRECHEEN

1

2

3

4

5

6

7

8

9

10

11

12

13

14

15

## CLOSE-UP OF BRECHEEN'S
## DELIVERY

1

2

3

4

5

6

7

**How Brecheen rolls off his curve ball**

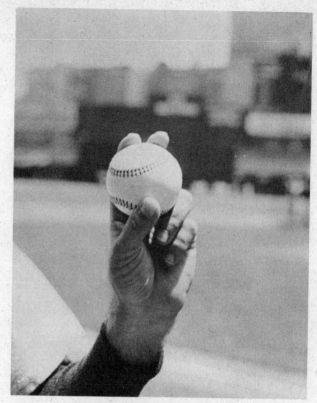

**"The Cat's" fast ball grip**

ing a screwball, he twists it in a reverse manner from that of his curve and with much less wrist snap. This also is delivered from a three-quarter or full delivery, whichever preferred.

Brecheen, in taking the full windup, uses virtually the same stance as Reynolds does. The sequence pictures, particularly those of the closeups of his screwball, accentuate his much higher kick as he rears back and coils his body to make the pitch. However, the same delicate balance and quick hop to a fielding position is noticeable.

Brecheen is one of the finest fielding pitchers in baseball—which is how he earned the nickname of "The Cat."

## FIELDING THE POSITION

Pop flies of sufficient height should be called for and taken by one of the infielders, the pitcher making certain that one of them is in command before moving out of the way. Hard-hit balls to the mound should be knocked down with the glove hand to avoid injury to the pitching hand, and, if time permits, the throw to base made in the normal motion.

A pitcher also should back up the crucial base on a throw from the outfield. If the throw is made to either third base or home, he should station himself in foul territory at a mid-way point in a position to back up either base.

With a man on third, the pitcher also covers home on pop flies near the plate and on balls which get away from the catcher. And one of his most important duties is to cover first base on all balls hit to the right side of the infield. On a ball hit deep to the first baseman, the pitcher's course, to avoid a col-

**Letting go of the screwball**

**Brecheen's pitching stance on the mound**

lision, is to the base path just short of the bag and then along the same course as the runner, tagging the bag with the right foot. On a ball hit wide of first, the pitcher heads directly to the base, steps on the right corner and holds his foot there while reaching for the throw, withdrawing his foot as quickly as possible to prevent accidental spiking.

## THE WARM-UP

This is another vital step—particularly for curve ball pitchers. No attempt should be made to put "stuff" on the ball until the pitching arm has been thoroughly loosened. The period should be for from ten to fifteen minutes, depending on the individual, lobbing the ball at first and gradually increasing the speed of the pitches. Curve balls or other breaking pitches should not be thrown until after at least five minutes of limbering the arm.

It is important to keep the arm warm between innings so that it doesn't tighten up and a half dozen pitches should be made, most of them without pressure, before facing a hitter.

If you take care of your arm, learn how to field your position and acquire a good working curve to go with any sort of a fast ball, you'll be a tough pitcher to beat in any league.

# 3. Pitching the Assortment

## As demonstrated by
## SAL MAGLIE
### New York Giants

"Pitching requires a little bit of talent —and an awful lot of hard work," explains Sal Maglie, whose league-leading twenty-three triumphs led the New York Giants to the National League pennant in 1951.

Part of this hard work is mastering a variety of pitches with which to confound the hitters. It is true that many successful hurlers make the grade with a fast ball, change up and curve.

Any Major Leaguer will tell you that the basic pitches discussed here are the ones to be brought under control first.

But there are a number of other deliveries which, if developed to a high degree, are just as effective. There have been numerous cases where, when a player's career was threatened by an arm injury, his playing days were prolonged beyond normal expectancy with a trick pitch. One such was Dutch Leonard, who undoubtedly lasted longer with a knuckle ball than he would have had his fast ball stayed with him.

These "extra" pitches, in addition to the knuckler, include the screwball, the fork ball and the palm ball. The pitcher who can mix one or two of these in with his basic pitches can be a big winner.

Such a master is Maglie, who has one of the most complete "mixtures" in the big leagues. Actually a curve ball specialist who can throw six different types of curves— fast, medium and slow from overhand and three-quarter overhand deliveries — the man they call "The Barber" knows how to handle every pitch in the books.

## THE KNUCKLE BALL

The knuckler is a pitch which has come into greater prominence during recent years through the effective work of Leonard, young Hoyt Wilhelm and others. This is one pitch which offers no strain in the arm and therefore has additional value, while its butterfly flight makes it particularly difficult for the batter to hit.

In the still photographs, Maglie shows how the knuckler is held by most knuckle-ball pitchers. This is done with the tips or nails of the first and second fingers resting on top of the ball while the ball is grasped firmly with the thumb and the third and fourth fingers. The ball may be delivered overhand

**Maglie's grip on the curve ball**

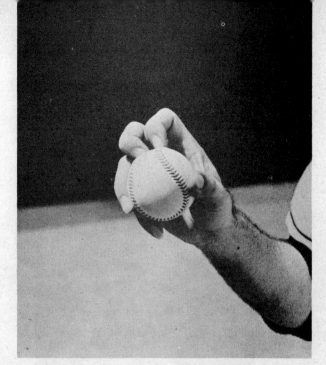

**Pushing off the knuckle ball**

**How Maglie holds the screwball**

**Maglie's stance on the mound**

## THE CHANGE UP, AS
## PITCHED BY SAL MAGLIE

1

2

3

4

5

6

7

**CLOSE-UP OF MAGLIE'S
DELIVERY**

1

2

3

4

5

6

7

8

9

10

11

12

13

14

15

from a three-quarter motion or sidearm with the fingers and wrist remaining stiff.

Some other pitchers prefer to place the first joint of the index and second finger on top of the ball, instead of the tips of the fingers. The ball then is delivered with considerable wrist snap, the bent fingers being extended as the ball is released. But for yourself, use the grip which is most comfortable.

## THE SCREWBALL

Maglie shows in the action sequence how he throws the screwball—actually a curve—breaking back to the side from which it was thrown. Pay particular attention to the manner in which his hand makes a swift quarter-turn inward, the opposite of a curve delivery, as the ball is released.

When the curve, because of the outward twist of the hand, rolls off the second finger, the action is completely reversed in the screwball. Here the wrist and hand snap is inward, using the same grip, and causing the ball to roll off the forefinger's inside edge as it emerges between the second and third fingers.

Thrown overhand, the screwball tends to break and drop. Once mastered, it is a dependable pitch but most pitchers warn against using it too often as it is likely to cause a strain on the arm.

It requires a very strong pitching arm and should not be attempted until after all the other pitches have been brought completely under control.

## THE FORK BALL

This is another "floater" like the knuckle ball and is held in a tripod between the thumb, first finger and second finger. The delivery is made as in the fast ball, with a forward wrist snap which slides the ball out between the spread index and middle finger. This pitch, like the knuckler, floats up to the plate before it breaks.

## THE PALM BALL

Even slower than the knuckler and the fork ball is the palm ball. This pitch is held in the palm with all the fingers on the ball. The pitch is made with an overhand delivery, the ball sliding from tl.umb and palm with no finger pressure and practically no wrist action.

Maglie, an artist at mixing up his pitches, urges particular attention to the closeup of his pitching stance on the rubber.

"Notice that my right foot is pointed outward when I take my stance," he says. "This means that it already is turned when I start my delivery and I get a much better push for the pitch."

This is one of the basic lessons, like learning to handle your fast ball and your curve. Only then is it time to dip into the assortment.

# 4. High Average Hitting

## As demonstrated by

## STAN MUSIAL

**St. Louis Cardinals**

There is a definite feeling among baseball men that batting stars are born, not made. But if you do not have exceptional talent, practice and you can develop it.

Proof of this is Stan Musial, who started out as a pitcher and only became the perennial batting champion of the National League after he hurt his pitching arm and was converted into an outfielder.

Stan the Man never has won the home run championship, although he hits his share of round-trippers. But he usually is the leader, or at least among the leaders, in total hits, doubles and triples—as well as that fat average.

Yet Musial's batting stance is not considered the perfect one, except by humiliated rival pitchers. It has been said that he stands at the plate like a man peeking around a corner. He can hit, and with amazing regularity.

How does a player do this? Not easily, but there are a number of points which can help boost that batting average. One of the most important is learning to hit to all fields. Another is to develop a good wrist snap. And very important, never take your eye off the ball from the time it leaves the pitcher's

hand and never use a bat which is too heavy for you.

Musial's exceptional number of extra base hits, doubles and triples, is due to a great extent to his fleet base running. This requires speed of foot which some players never can develop. But to have a chance for those extra bases, he still had to hit safely.

There are two methods of hitting to all fields, both important for boosting your average. One is the manner in which the bat is swung and the other is anticipating medium-speed pitches.

For example, a left-handed hitter following through with the regular wrist snap would hit to right field. If he refuses to alter his swing, he would hit there consistently and a defense might be tightened as was done against Ted Williams by moving the shortstop over into the right side of the infield. This reduces his chances of getting a hit although in Williams' case, he lashed the ball so savagely that even the defense couldn't stop him all the time.

But a left-handed hitter who occasionally hits to left field keeps the defense scattered. This can be accomplished by swinging late or reducing the wrist snap so much that the

## FULL BODY VIEW OF MUSIAL'S SWING

1

2

3

4

5

6

7

## CLOSE UP OF
## MUSIAL'S SWING

1

2

3

4

5

6

7

**How Musial grips the bat**

hands are out ahead of the bat when the ball is met.

Another aid is in expecting a medium-speed pitch when you try to "guess" what the pitcher will throw. In that manner, the swing will be late for a fast ball and thus push it to the opposite field, while it will be early for slow balls or curves and will pull them to the side from which the player is hitting.

The bat you use is very important. If it is too heavy it will ruin your timing. It should be held with the hands close together, as Musial demonstrates in his grip. But whether you use the end grip, with the hands at the end or an inch or so from the end, or the choke grip, with the hands several inches from the end, is not too important when it comes to hitting regularly. The end grip simply increases your long distance power.

Nor is the stance particularly important, except in certain points, as long as you feel comfortable up at the plate. As proof, there is a wide variety of batting stances in use in the majors.

Generally, however, there are certain "must" points to be noted in the sequence photos of Musial's swing.

First, in taking the stance, Musial's shoulders and hips are in line, his knees are slightly bent and his weight is distributed evenly on both feet.

The bat is held high and, as the pitcher starts his delivery, note the cocking of the hands. By this time, the weight has almost entirely been shifted to the back leg, only the toes of the front foot maintaining Musial's balance. This permits him to delay his step, another factor in hitting to all fields.

It is best to hold the bat high because it is easier to drop it into low pitches than to raise it for high ones. Also a downward swing is more effective as it increases the prospects of a line drive.

Musial's swing is a symphony of smoothness and fine wrist action. Note that his hands have already reached the hitting zone when he applies the wrist whip. As the bat swings through, his weight has been transferred to the front foot and he is pushing with the toes of his rear foot as the body leans in the direction in which the ball has been hit. This is to give full driving power and, as insurance Musial pivots until the bat has been carried far to the rear of his body.

To sum up methods in which you may improve your average:

Hit to all fields by swinging as if all pitches were of medium speed delivery and learn to both push and pull the ball;

Develop a downward line drive-swing;

Don't use a bat too heavy for you;

Keep your eye on the ball all the way, then use a comfortable stance and swing smoothly.

# 5. Home Run Hitting

## As demonstrated by
## RALPH KINER

**Chicago Cubs**

You don't have to be a giant to hit home runs—but it helps. It stands to reason that a strapping, powerful man with co-ordination can hit a ball farther than a short man of less strength.

Yet many of the biggest players in the major leagues rarely hit home runs with any steadiness, while some of the smallest have with amazing regularity. One such was Mel Ott of the New York Giants. Only five feet, nine inches, weighing 160 pounds, he won the National League home run title six times.

Ott accomplished this primarily by learning to pull the ball with almost fantastic marksmanship into the short right field stands at the Polo Grounds. That was a striking feat of adaptation.

Yet your home run champions usually are husky men who are able to bludgeon the ball out of the park on sheer power alone. One of the greatest is Ralph Kiner, perennial home run king of the National League. A two-hundred pounder who stands a sinewy six feet, two inches, Kiner has all the attributes needed for home run greatness. Here he demonstrates his super-swing, the form which has

written so much baseball history.

It is, for those with the necessary strength, an excellent model to emulate if you want to hit baseball's thrill blow. For Kiner's is the perfect uppercut swing favored by the muscular, long-ball hitters.

As Ralph takes his stance in the batter's box, note how he stands with his rear foot just back of the plate. His feet are about parallel and equi-distant from the line of the plate, with the front foot pointed slightly outward in a partially open stance. Some batters like to move forward in the batting box when hitting against slow-ball or sinker pitchers, moving to the rear of the box against fast overhand hurlers.

Kiner carries his bat unusually high, with the back elbow slightly below the shoulder. As the pitcher begins his delivery, note the cocking of the wrists and then the rear elbow dropping as the bat starts down. Meanwhile, Kiner has started his stride, but the front foot is not planted firmly until he proves where the pitch is going, thus helping to preserve his timing.

**KINER'S FAMOUS
HOME RUN SWING**

1

2

3

4

5

6

7

**CLOSE-UP OF
KINER'S SWING**

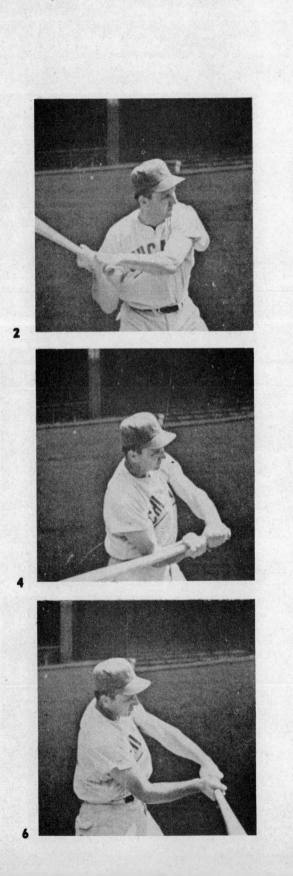

1

2

3

4

5

6

7

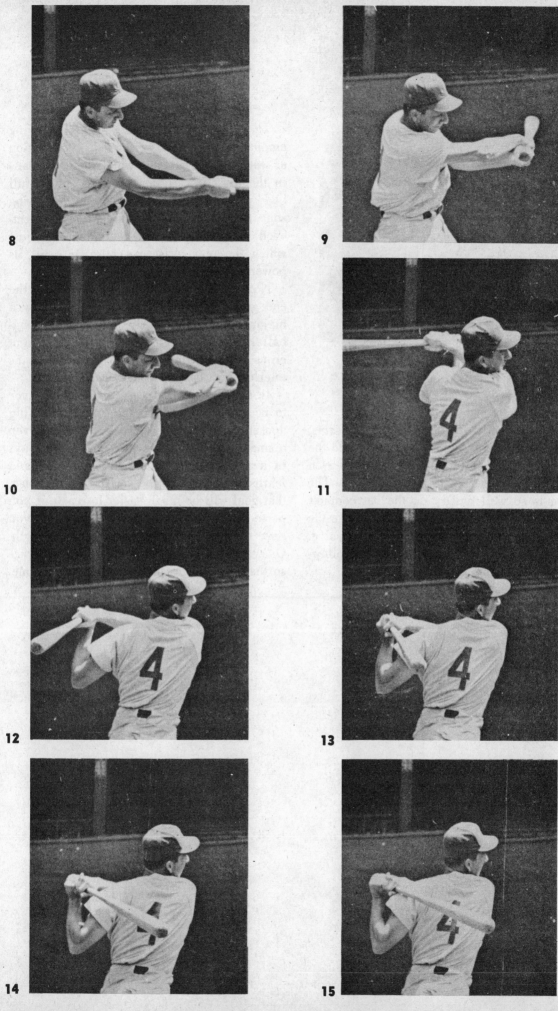

**Kiner's grip on the bat**

Next, notice the co-ordinating of arms, shoulders and hips as his weight shifts to the forward leg and, with the hands already even with the plate, he begins his wrist lash. The swing is so well timed that the bat contacts the ball out in front of the plate, before the break of the ball can become fully effective. It is after the ball is hit that the follow-through wrist roll is easily discerned.

The closeups of Kiner's powerful swing emphasize the fine wrist and hand action as well as the manner in which his body leans in the direction of the swing to assure full body power. As the bat whips into the hitting zone, the arm toward the pitcher has straightened out and is providing a solid base against which the rear wrist can push with all its power.

Note how close Ralph's hands are in the end grip. This is the one most favored by a majority of hitters, particularly of the long-ball group, although there have been numerous batters with such grip peculiarities as interlocking, hands apart, etc.

In summation, the odds are in your favor to become a home run hitter if you are big and strong. But, as proved by Mel Ott, even a small man can attain that goal if he plays in a park where the corners are close and learns to shoot for the nearest spots. Also, that goal will be much easier to reach, if you perfect your timing to such a degree that you have the full advantage of all your strength. One last suggestion: Learn to whip the wrists so the bat explodes through the hitting zone.

# 6. Switch-Hitting

## As demonstrated by
## MICKEY MANTLE
### New York Yankees

The switch-hitter is an extremely valuable man to any team and, in an era of two-platoon baseball, will find that the ability to hit from either side of the plate can be one of his greatest playing assets.

It is easily seen that a left-handed hitter has the edge on a right-handed hitter when there is a right-handed pitcher on the mound, and vice versa, a right-handed hitter has an edge against a left-handed pitcher. Thus, in an age of specialists, there are many batters used only against southpaws or exclusively against right-handers.

"With a power-hitter of the switch type, you don't have to worry about the character of the opposition hurling," asserts Casey Stengel, the immortal manager of the New York Yankees.

He should know, because he came up with one of the best of all time—and possibly the greatest—in Mickey Mantle, who demonstrates his fine swing.

There have been many switch-hitters, or turnabout-hitters, in the major leagues. The early ones included Frankie Frisch, Buzz Arlett, Dave Bancroft, Mark Koenig, Wally Schang, Max Carey, Herb Pennock and Ted

Lyons. Of the present era, Red Schoendienst, Sam Jethroe, Ebba St. Claire, Steve Gromek, Early Wynn, Ted Gray and Russ Meyer are just a few well known switch-hitters.

But Mantle, hailed as one of the great young hitters, is the most explosive switch-hitter in baseball annals. On April 9, 1953, at an exhibition game in Pittsburgh's Forbes Field, he smacked a towering drive of better than 400 feet over the 90-foot high right field wall. He was batting left-handed.

On April 17, 1953, at Griffith Stadium in Washington, Mantle smashed a homer over the center field wall. It was a drive measured at 565 feet. This time he was batting right-handed.

Usually a switch-hitter has his power from his basic, original stance. Whether he is batting right-handed or left-handed, Mantle's stance is almost identical. Most switch-hitters hit better from one side than they do from the other. Yet of the first 14 homers Mantle hit in 1952, he had seven from *each* side. At Joplin in 1950, he hit 26 homers—14 left-handed and 12 right-handed.

There is no definite record of who first tried switch-hitting, but it is believed to have

**MANTLE'S "ADOPTED"
LEFTHANDED SWING**

1

2

3

4

5

6

7

8

9

10

11

12

13

14

15

**CLOSE-UP OF THE SWING**

**MANTLE "LEARNED"**

1

2

3

4

5

6

7

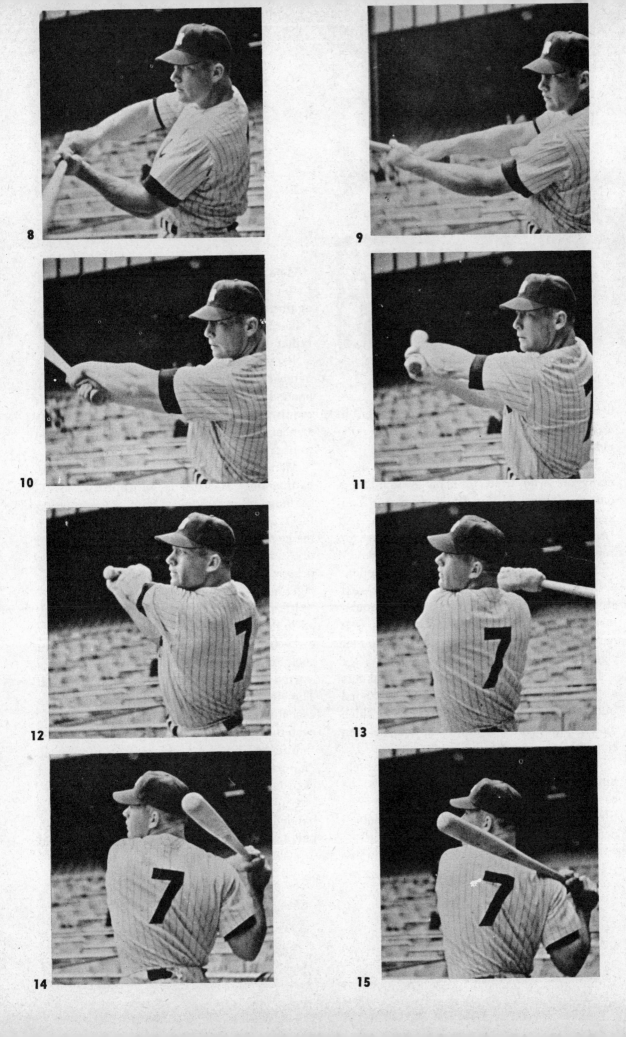

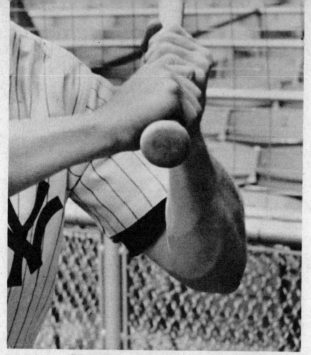

**Mantle's grip on the bat**

occurred when some unidentified player, in a slump, tried to hit from his opposite side out of sheer desperation.

It is a known fact that there have been managers who tried to make switch-hitters out of players. Miller Huggins of the Yankees, a switch-hitter himself, tried to convert Leo Durocher when the light-hitting shortstop reported in 1928, but it didn't take.

Yet there are other managers who oppose a batter's shifting unless he can show real ability in what might be called the "unnatural" stance. Just about every batter has a natural location at the plate. He is either right-handed or left-handed.

However, if the batter discovers a weakness as a right-handed batter against right-handed pitching, and boasts the adaptability which makes it possible for him to switch, he then can become a switch-hitter.

Mantle's experiences in becoming a switch-hitter indicates that the younger you are, the easier it will be for you to master this versatile method of batting before you fit into a decided one-way batting groove.

As a youngster, Mickey was a right-handed batter exclusively. Then he began to hit against his father and his grandfather. His father was a right-handed pitcher; his grandfather left-handed.

Because it obviously is easier for a left-handed batter to follow the pitch of a right-handed pitcher, Mickey began to switch. It required patience but soon, using the same stance from both sides, he could hit equally well from either side.

Managers are inclined to encourage switch-batting only if there is an approach to expertness in both stances. But, substantiating the records, you will note no weaknesses in the sequence pictures of Mantle's left-handed or "unnatural" swing, which has the same perfect balance and power as his natural, or right-handed swing.

Like the other long-distance hitters included in this book, the complete lack of strain or awkwardness is noticeable. Study the extra cock of the wrists just before the swing is started and the smooth pivot into the ball. The closeup pictures of Mantle's swing again accentuate the perfect rhythm of his swing, even though this is from his "unnatural" side.

Mickey perfected the chance from his "natural" side at such an early age that not even he knows which is his best batting side, but in 1951 he looked so good batting left-handed that Stengel contemplated having him bat from that side exclusively. This, mind you, despite the fact that Mantle originally and naturally was a right-handed hitter.

Switch-hitting as a regular procedure is almost a lost art in baseball. Nobody seems to know quite why, although the main reason may be that the players do not work hard enough on their "unnatural" swing to become proficient. But, as Mantle proves, if a player begins early enough, the adaptation can be made and with highly satisfactory results.

Undoubtedly the age of the baseball specialists is here to stay. High speed modern baseball demands that every advantage be taken — such as using right-handed hitters against left-handed pitchers at every opportunity. That's the reason for two-platoon baseball which keeps many fine players sitting on the bench just about half the time.

But there is no logical reason to keep a fine switch-hitter like Mantle out of the game regardless of the side the pitches are coming from.

It is a skill, however, which requires determination, ambition and practice. Start at an early age—and keep at it until hitting either way feels "natural."

# 7. Pull-Hitting

## As demonstrated by
## HANK SAUER
### Chicago Cubs

Most players are pull-hitters, which means that a right-handed batter "pulls" the ball around to the left field side or a left-handed batter "pulls" the ball around to the right field side.

The "pull," which can be controlled so the ball travels close to the foul line, is of particular value. Such hits are most difficult to handle by the outfielders and, in many parks, that is the closest point to the stands for a home run. As pointed out before, it was Mel Ott's ability to "pull" the ball into the close right field stands which won so many home run championships for him when he was with the New York Giants.

One of the best pull-hitters is Hank Sauer, the National League's most valuable player of 1952, who demonstrates the terrific wrist, arm and shoulder work necessary to pull the ball. A major factor in good pull-hitting is clearly evident in these split-second action pictures of Sauer's swing. That is, the early planting of the forward foot, almost before the arms have started their swing.

Some other types of hitters, it should be pointed out, delay their forward step until it can be timed with the pitch, but Sauer and most other top pull-hitters take their step early and plant their weight solidly as they start their swing.

Because they are set early, pull-hitters are in better position to hit a fast ball than are other types of batters. Most of them are "fast ball-guessers," or batters who anticipate a fast ball most of the time. The inclination, therefore, is to be off balance for slow or breaking deliveries.

The batting (note Sauer's swing) is done mostly with the arms. This is necessary because the body does not swing its weight at the same time the wrists and arms begin their swing. The hips and legs swing first and the upper body follows.

Sauer, who is six feet, four inches in height, is a particularly effective pull-hitter, and his extreme size and strength proved it when in 1952 he tied Ralph Kiner for the National League home run championship. Note the terrific "pull" of his arms and shoulders in his swing.

See how he seems to lean back away from the pitch as he pulls his arms around into the

**Sauer's grip on the bat**

ball and then supplies added power with a fine follow-through.

## HITTING TO THE OPPOSITE FIELD

One of the most important things for the pull-hitter to learn is to hit to the opposite field. This is necessary so that the batter will not hit to the same spot all the time and thus permit the defense to bunch on him. By occasionally hitting to the opposite field he can keep the defense "loose."

"You can't change your stance to do this or you will tip off the defense," Sauer explains. "You must use your regular stance and change your batting style, hitting to the opposite field with your hands and arms."

This is done by keeping the hands out in front of the swing when the ball is contacted, instead of pulling the bat on around, or by swinging a bit late at the pitch so that the ball is met before the bat is whipped all the way around.

Even a normal spray-hitter can and should learn to pull the ball, as it is a valuable asset to any batter. It is in many parks the closest route to the home run. Even if the ball doesn't make it all the way to the stands, it would be difficult for the outfielders to handle when it drops in along the foul line.

**SAUER "PULLING"**

**THE BALL**

2

4

6

1

3

5

7

## CLOSE-UP OF SAUER'S "PULL" ACTION

1

2

3

4

5

6

7

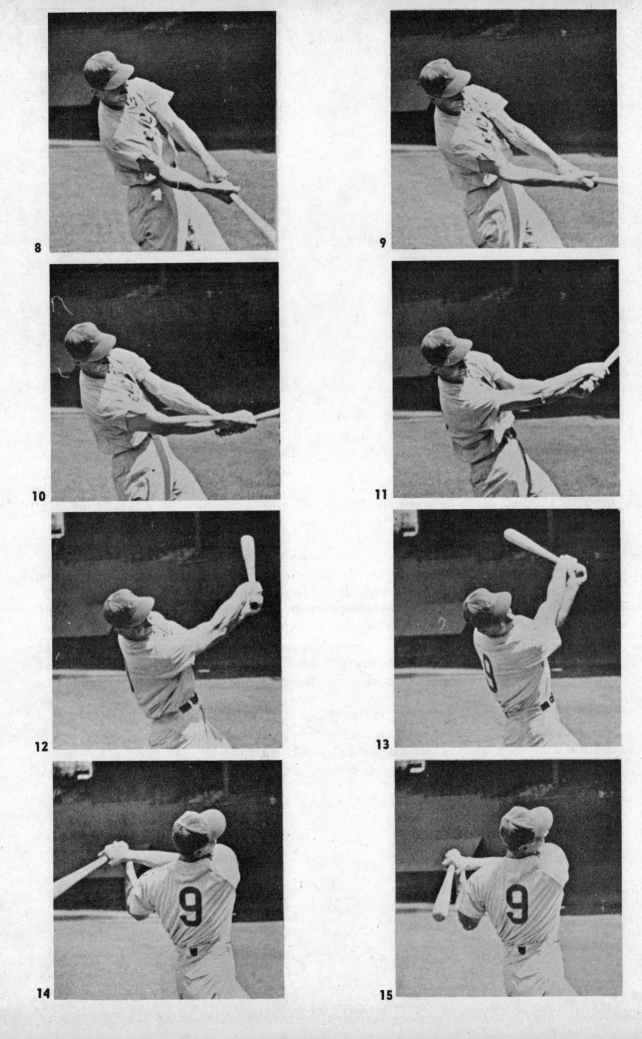

# 8. The Bunt

## As demonstrated by
## PHIL RIZZUTO
### New York Yankees

The bunt is the big weapon for the little man. The supersluggers of baseball seldom take the time or interest to master it fully.

Most of the small men in the big leagues are extremely fast. They know they can't depend on slugging power to move the men around the bases and so they perfect the bunt which does most of the work for them. It is one of the reasons why smaller-statured men like Nelson Fox, Peewee Reese and Richie Ashburn have attained stardom. It also explains why shortstop Phil Rizzuto of the New York Yankees became one of the greatest baseball players of all time. For Rizzuto, although, only five feet, six inches in height, admits that bunting is "one of my bread-and-butter" talents."

There are two different types of bunts— the sacrifice bunt and the offensive bunt. Each is hit in a different way, as you will see in the action pictures of Rizzuto's bunting styles.

## THE SACRIFICE BUNT

This bunt is designed to advance the base runner. It usually is anticipated, so no deception is required. The principal idea is to achieve a bunt which the pitcher or infielders will have difficulty handling so that, while the batter may be an easy out, the base runners will be certain to advance.

"I take my regular stance at the plate but bring my rear foot forward just before the ball is released by the pitcher," says Rizzuto, one of the finest bunters in the game. "I hold the bat loosely so the ball won't be hit too hard and I try to guide the ball away from the pitcher to be certain he won't be able to make a play on the runners. I like to place my bunt close enough to the foul line so both the pitcher and the fielder will make a try for it."

In the sequence pictures of Rizzuto mak-

# RIZZUTO LAYS DOWN A SACRIFICE BUNT

# CLOSE-UP OF THE SACRIFICE

**RIZZUTO BUNTING FOR A BASE HIT**

**CLOSE-UP OF RIZZUTO'S BASE HIT BUNT**

ing a sacrifice bunt, note how he suits the action to his words. Before the ball is on its way, he has brought his rear foot around so his body is squarely facing the pitcher, weight on the balls of his feet. Meanwhile, the bottom hand remains in its regular place on the bat handle, but the top hand has started a slide up the barrel until that hand is holding the bat near the trademark and only by the fingertips.

While Rizzuto is shifting his weight to his right leg to get set for a running start, note that he does not move from his position until after he is certain the ball has been hit. If the run is started before the ball is hit, it is possible that, because of the momentum of the bat, the ball will be popped up or struck too hard, causing a double-play.

## BUNTING FOR A BASE-HIT

Here the batter is on his own, and he must pick his spot. Rizzuto prefers to lay one down when he is having a bad day at the plate or is riding a slump. A bunt also is effective if the infielders are playing deep or if the pitcher is throwing slow stuff. But it requires complete deception so that the pitcher or infielders cannot anticipate it.

Rizzuto demonstrates his short bunt down the third base line in the action sequence. To make certain that the deception is prolonged, he takes his regular batting stance — and maintains it until after the pitcher has released the ball. He doesn't square off in the position taken to assure accuracy for the

sacrifice. Instead, he quickly slides his rear foot back, away from the plate, and slides his upper hand down on the bat all in the same motion.

The ball seems almost to be past him when it is contacted, for he has pushed the bat handle back with his lower hand and already has started running as the ball is contacted. This method assures him a fast getaway and is particularly effective against deep-playing third baseman.

"If I want to send the ball to the first base side," Phil explains, "I push the ball out that way. This is done by pushing the arms out in the direction of first base as the batter begins to run in that direction. The bunt should be aimed between the pitcher and first baseman or close to the foul line."

The most difficult bunt is the squeeze. This is used only when a run is needed badly and its success depends completely on surprise. For once the squeeze is called, usually with no more than one out, the ball must be hit or the base runner will be trapped off third base.

Much depends on the runner in this play, too, because if he starts for the plate before the pitch is delivered, the pitcher will throw a ball which can't be hit by the batter and the runner will be trapped.

Except for the sacrifice, the success of a bunt depends entirely on its surprise. The odds are on your side if you can learn to bunt skillfully and pick the right moment to deliver. You are out, of course, if you bunt on third strike and the ball goes foul. Thus the defense ordinarily draws back after two strikes. That's when, many times, big league batters will gamble and lay it down again, counting on their bunting to pay off. Getting the right kind of pitch, in this case, is extremely important.

"At the start of a game," Rizzuto says, "I try to learn what the pitcher is throwing. The best pitches to bunt are curves and let-up fast balls because there is less chance of popping up."

Bunting, like everything else in baseball, is conquered only by patient practice and hard work. But once mastered, it is a priceless asset. The slugger who can bunt will hit for dizzy averages, but all too many of them neglect it. That's why it is known as the big weapon for the little man, and few ever make the major league grade without it.

# 9. Catching

## As demonstrated by
## CLINT COURTNEY
### Baltimore Orioles

Catching is one of the toughest jobs in baseball, so demanding, in fact, that the catcher's equipment has been called the "tools of ignorance."

Actually a catcher, in addition to being game and courageous, must be clever, too. For most of the time it is the catcher who is running the ball club and telling the pitcher what to throw. The man who aimed at becoming a good catcher had the foresight to choose this position because he knew able receivers are always in great demand.

One of the most able and courageous in the major leagues is Clint Courtney, who demonstrates some of the finer points of the catcher's arts.

His chores are many, but first note the stance, which Courtney shows in his full-length picture. Crouched behind the plate, perfect balance is necessary to cope with any emergency. The feet, with knees apart, are very nearly parallel in the position taken to give the signal to the pitcher. The glove hand is extended out beyond the left knee to hide the signal from the third base coaching box. The right arm is on the right thigh, with the

hand bent inward to signal.

After having given the sign, the catcher moves forward and crouches as close as possible to the plate without interfering with the batter's swing. Here again the feet are kept parallel so that a shift may be made to either side.

Note the manner in which Courtney's hands work when catching a high pitch or a low pitch. On a high pitch, the ball is caught with fingers up and thumbs close together. On a low pitch, the glove is swung around so the heels of the hands are together. But as the pitch starts, the hands are always held in the fingers-up, thumbs-together position so the pitch will not be tipped.

Watch how Courtney's ungloved hand moves out slightly ahead of the glove. Then, as the ball hits the glove, the fingers swiftly cover the ball so it will not bounce out. A rapid twist of the mitt allows the ball to drop into the fingers and facilitate a quick throw, if necessary.

Using the balanced catching position, with both feet parallel, the body is balanced to move easily to either side of the plate for

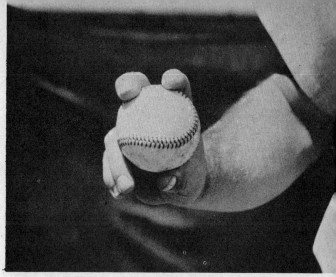

**Courtney's grip throwing to the bases**

**Blocking home plate**

## FIELDING THE BALL

wide throws. Very wide ones are stopped by throwing the body toward the ball while low balls are blocked by dropping to one knee or to both knees.

## CATCHING POP FLIES

Another difficult feat is catching fly balls near the plate or behind the plate. One aid is that a right-handed hitter usually lifts the ball to the right side and a left-handed hitter ordinarily pops to the left side. He also should take the lofted balls immediately in front of the plate, as most fields are laid out so the sun is not in the batter's eyes—and therefore not in the catcher's eyes.

Getting rid of the mask so it will not be a hindrance is another "must" for the catcher to learn. On a fly ball near the plate the catcher locates the flight of the ball and then flings the mask out of the way. If the ball is far from the plate, the mask is shoved to the back of the head with the thumb and falls back out of the way.

## FIELDING THE BALL

The mask also is pushed over the back of the head when fielding a bunt or slowly-rolling topped ball just in front of the plate. In this case, the ball is fielded by sweeping the hands together with the gloved hand in front of the ball and the bare hand to the rear of its line of flight. The fielding always is done with the body facing first base to keep the play in the catcher's vision.

## THROWING

Courtney, in a still photo, displays the grip he uses to throw the ball. The throw itself is done overhand and is snapped from the shoulder to the pitcher in such a manner that only a little more force would carry it on to second base. A catcher must develop a strong arm—and use it without hesitation.

Only in this manner can he prevent stolen bases from becoming a losing habit. No matter who is on base, it is a good policy to keep reminding yourself that he might run. If you are certain that the base runner is going to go, call for a pitchout—a wide pitch at which the batter cannot swing and which gives you plenty of room to throw to a base.

As for the throw itself, never drop the arm below shoulder level. When the pitch is caught, bring the arm straight up and throw the ball on a line to the base. In that way there is no lost motion which would occur if the arm were brought around in a circle. The ball is fired away better and has smoother carry.

Still another chore for the alert catcher is backing up first base when there is nobody on or when there is only a man on first, although in the latter case, he would have to hustle back to his post to protect the plate. He also covers first and third base when there is nobody on base and the ball is hit to those positions.

All in all, it is a tough position. Therefore, the man who can play it well is in great demand.

# 10. First Base

## As demonstrated by
## GIL HODGES
**Brooklyn Dodgers**

Two of the most important qualifications for a first baseman are to be able to make the "big stretch" and to be a high-class fielder.

No other player on the team is called upon to make as many defensive plays as the first baseman and he must be able to handle a wide variety of throws. He must go high for the ball or dig it out of the dirt; he must go wide to his left or his right. The distance of his stretch often is the difference between a runner being safe or out; he must also cover his own territory as well.

One of the best in the big leagues is towering Gil Hodges of the Brooklyn Dodgers. Six feet, two inches tall, the Indiana strong man here demonstrates how he stretches to meet the ball on those trigger close plays where inches mean the difference between victory and defeat.

Hodges shows how to make the stretch on a normal play from shortstop or third base. Notice his stance in front of the bag as the infielder plays the ball. His weight is balanced unevenly on both feet, permitting him to shift his position at the last moment. In the case of this normal throw from the left side of the infield, the throw already is underway as Gil slides the right foot back to the bag and steps forward with his left leg in a giant stride. Then he leans forward as far as possible to meet the ball, the rear leg being drawn away from the bag as soon as the catch is made so he will be out of the runner's way.

The reason for the late shift from the ready stance is that on throws to the right field side of the bag, the left foot is slid back to the bag and the right foot takes the forward stride. This keeps perfect body balance.

When a throw is very wide of the bag, a crossover step is used, as this permits a longer step. Thus, on a wide throw to the right field side of the bag, the right foot holds the bag while the left leg crosses over and out. If the throw is to the plate side of first, the bag is held with the left leg and the crossover is made with the right leg. When a throw is high, the first baseman goes up for the ball and then makes the tag with the foot closest to the bag.

# HODGES DEMONSTRATES THE BIG STRETCH

In cases where the catcher, pitcher or third baseman fields a ball in front of the plate, the first baseman keeps his left foot on the bag and reaches out with his right foot toward shortstop, meanwhile giving the thrower a target by holding his cupped hands out at shoulder level to the second base side of the head. If the third strike rolls behind the catcher, permitting the batter to run, the same stance is taken in foul territory, with the right foot on the bag and the target hands are cupped to the side of the head away from the diamond. This helps the thrower to avoid hitting the runner.

## FIELDING THE POSITION

The batter's ability comes into consideration, as well as the type of ball hit, when determining how much ground a first baseman covers. For instance, the territory is larger against a right-handed pull-hitter than a left-handed pull-hitter. In the former, the second baseman is playing closer to second base and the first baseman must play farther off the bag.

On balls which are hit close to the foul line, the first baseman runs toward the bag in fair territory and tags the bag with his left foot to avoid contact with the base runner, meanwhile warning away the pitcher with a shout or a wave of the hand. On runs to the bag from a short first base position, the first baseman continues on across the bag into foul territory if he can safely keep out of the runner's path. On close plays, it is better to slide into the bag, touching only the infield side and withdrawing the foot as soon

as possible.

If the ball is hit short up the first base line, the batter may be tagged or the play may be made to the pitcher who covers first. With a runner on third, the runner who stops must be run down quickly. In cases where the pitcher covers first, an underhand toss letter-high is made to the pitcher. On longer throws, the ball must be thrown to the bag.

## HANDLING BUNTS

In bunt situations, the first baseman races toward the batter as the pitcher throws. If the ball is bunted hard, the play can be made to second base to catch the advancing runner if there is one. But on slow-rolling bunts, the play is made to first base, where the bag is covered by the second baseman.

## HOLDING THE RUNNER

When the runner must be held close to first base, the first baseman takes a position in front of the bag, facing the pitcher, with the left foot near the foul line and the right foot just in front of the corner of the bag. If the runner is slow and the batter is likely to hit to the right side of the infield, the first baseman takes a position slightly in back of the runner.

Defensively, the first baseman also must back up second base on all throws from the left side with no one on base. He must cover second base if it is unguarded, and cover home plate on pop flies and rundowns in which the catcher is involved.

# 11. Second Base

## As demonstrated by
## JUNIOR GILLIAM
**Brooklyn Dodgers**

The second baseman must cover ground, field skillfully, and be able to get off short throws with swiftness and accuracy as well as make the double-play.

One of the most promising young second basemen in the major leagues is Junior Gilliam of the Brooklyn Dodgers, who here demonstrates both phases of the double-play — making the forceout at second and the throw to first, and starting the twin-killing by throwing to the converging shortstop.

Gilliam's work over the bag is swift with no lost motion. As the shortstop fields the ball, he begins his move to the bag. Note in the sequence pictures how he is in motion as the ball comes to him, his left foot just short of the bag.

This enables him to stride over the bag with his right foot and plant it firmly for the pivot and the throw. Then, as the body winds up for the quick relay of the ball to first, in the same motion he drags his left foot across

the bag for the forceout. As he throws to first, his stride already has carried him to the inside of the base line so he is out of the way of the base runner who would try to break up the double-play. This gives him a clear view for his throw to first.

There are several other methods of making the forceout and the throw to first for the double-play.

One of them is to step on the bag with the left foot and then on over the bag with the right foot for the throw, which is much .the same as Gilliam's method.

Other second basemen prefer to step on the bag with the left foot as the ball is taken and then to push back onto the right leg for the throw. Still others take the ball with the right foot on the bag and throw directly from there, pushing back to the left leg and the outside of the base path out of the runner's way after the throw is made.

Generally, a second baseman arriving at

# STARTING THE DOUBLE PLAY AT SECOND BASE

the bag late must continue on across the bag while other methods may be used if he has time to get set.

## FIELDING THE POSITION

The second baseman's chief fielding concern is the area between first base and second base, or as much of it as he can safely handle. The more he can cover, the less risky ball-handling there will be between the fielding first baseman and a covering pitcher. The first baseman permits the second baseman to take anything he can reach, thus giving the first baseman time to get back and cover the bag.

With first base occupied, speed is essential. In the action pictures of Gilliam fielding the ball and starting the double-play, he first makes certain to dig out the ball and then swiftly gets it away.

The second baseman covers second base on all balls that are hit to the left side of the infield or on fly balls to the left side. He also must cover first base on sacrifice bunts and when the first baseman leaves the bag to take a fly ball.

It also is part of the second baseman's duties to back up both first base and second base in certain situations. He must back up first base on throws made from near the plate and must back up second when the shortstop takes throws from the pitcher, catcher or left field.

Summing up, the second baseman, as in the case of the shortstop, must be, above all, a nimble fielder but doesn't necessarily have to be a power-hitter to earn his way. And his main job is handling one of the team's key defensive positions. Many light-hitters make the major league grade purely on their brilliant fielding ability. Neither size nor strength is as important here as the ability to be a defensive standout.

# 12. Shortstop

## As demonstrated by
## PEEWEE REESE
### Brooklyn Dodgers

The shortstop must have the same qualities as the second baseman — ability to cover ground and to field skillfully. But a top-notch shortstop's arm meets more of a test because his throw, while longer to first base, should have the same snap and accuracy.

The most important chore of the shortstop, key man in the infield, is to be able to make the double-play. One of the greatest in the annals of the game is Peewee Reese, whose work at short led the Brooklyn Dodgers to numerous National League pennants.

Reese, who here demonstrates the short-stop's method on both ends of the double-play, is another of those fellows like Rizzuto and Gilliam who prove you do not have to be a physical giant to become a major league star. Only five feet, nine inches, Peewee displays the smoothness and ability which proves that real baseball class quite often comes in small packages.

Speed is essential in completing the double-play, for the flip to second to force the runner from first must be done quickly in order to give the relay-thrower time to get the ball over to first. Reese shows how he makes the scoop- or shovel-throw to the second baseman covering second base in the double-play. You will see that the ball is first fielded cleanly with both hands.

Make certain that you have the ball securely before attempting to throw, in order to avoid costly errors. Notice how Reese takes the ball with both hands, the bare hand quickly covering the ball as it hits the glove. Almost in the same instant, the bare hand takes a grip on the ball, and in one motion, the ball is picked from the glove and tossed with a smooth underhand motion. The ball is aimed shoulder-high, and directly at the bag, so that the second baseman can take it in stride.

**REESE STARTING THE DOUBLE PLAY AT SHORTSTOP**

On longer throws, of course, the ball can be whipped side arm to the second baseman. But on most throws to first, the shortstop straightens up if time permits and throws in his normal manner to the first baseman to insure a more accurate throw.

Most shortstops, when acting as the middle man in the double-play, take the ball in stride, as Reese is doing in the action pictures of his pivot and throw to first base. Note how Reese is just short of the bag with his right foot and plants the left foot next to the outside corner of the bag as he takes the ball. This permits him to drag his right foot across the bag as he hops to the outside of the base line out of the way of a base runner who would try to break up the double-play. As the hop carries him to the outside of the base line, Peewee shifts his weight to his right leg and, in one smooth motion, fires the ball to first.

Other shortstops like to step directly on the bag with the right foot and then take a long step with the left to begin their hop on the outside of the base path.

When the shortstop has been playing deep and sees that he will arrive at the bag too late to step across in front of the runner, the bag can be tagged with the left foot and the step for the throw to first is then made to the in-field side of the bag with the right foot.

## FIELDING THE POSITION

Second base is covered by the shortstop on all balls hit to the right field side of the diamond. He also covers third base when the third baseman is fielding a ball out of position and when the third baseman acts as the cutoff man on a throw from the outfield.

The shortstop's duties also include backing up second base when the second baseman takes throws from the catcher or pitcher or right fielder. He must back up third base, too, on throws to the third baseman from the catcher.

A good shortstop and a pitcher also can work out an effective pick-off play against a runner on second base, but this is a highly difficult and risky technique and calls for long practice before being attempted.

This position, as well as second base, is the spot for the nimble little man with the sure pair of hands. Learn to field those hot smashes, never taking your eye off the ball. Learn to perform that hop pivot on the double-play and to throw surely and swiftly from almost any position and even if you lack size, you can have the qualities for the major leagues.

# 13. Third Base

## As demonstrated by
## GIL McDOUGALD
**New York Yankees**

Playing the "hot corner" is one of the most difficult assignments in baseball, for the third baseman must be able to block those hot smashes down the line, move in fast on bunts and slow-rolling balls and make the long throw to first base.

One of the game's finest fielding third basemen who, because of these assets, rose rapidly to stardom with the New York Yankees, is Gil McDougald, who here demonstrates his form in stopping a hard smash which can be fielded cleanly.

"Most of the time they come so fast that you have to stop them any way you can," McDougald explains. "The best way is to get your feet together and be sure you stop the ball with some part of your body. If you manage to knock down a hot one you still have time to grab it and make a play on the runner."

McDougald illustrates the method of taking a hot smash with a good bounce so that the ball can be thrown swiftly to first base. Notice that he times the ball so the weight of his body is shifting to his left leg just as he makes the catch with both hands. The ball is picked out of the glove for the throw as he

makes a quick little hop on his left foot to get the throw away quickly.

On slow-rolling balls, the third baseman must cover the entire area between the pitching mound and third base. This is because he usually plays much closer to the plate than the shortstop, to protect against bunts. Thus, on balls hit toward the shortstop, the third baseman often cuts in front of the shortstop and takes the ball with a gloved-hand pickup. Otherwise, on slow rollers, the shortstop might not get to the ball in time to make a play on the batter.

Many times the third baseman could reach a harder hit ball traveling directly toward the shortstop. But the shortstop must be allowed to take the ball, if he calls for it, because the third baseman might deflect it away from both of them. The reason for permitting the shortstop to take this kind of ball is that he is in better position to take the throw.

The majority of bunts are made up the third base line and, in fielding them, the third baseman uses both hands unless the ball has almost stopped rolling. This is to prevent the ball kicking away because of the twist it may have. If the ball is barely moving, however,

# McDOUGALD STOPPING A HOT CORNER SMASH

it can be picked up with the bare hand for a faster throw.

Immediately after making a throw, the third baseman must return to his base to cover it. This is his first duty with a man on first and the third baseman fielding a ball. Otherwise, the runner may advance all the way from first base to third base.

The third baseman acts as the cutoff man on hits to extreme left field. The remainder of the time when the cutoff is being used, the shortstop takes the ball. Then it is the third baseman's duty to call the cutoff play, advising the shortstop whether to cut off the ball. If the throw to the plate can catch the base runner, he tells the shortstop to let the ball go. If the runner cannot be caught by the throw, he advises the shortstop to cut it off.

It is the third baseman's duty not only to back up second base when throws are made from right field, barring the possibility of a play at third base, but also to back up the pitcher on throws from first base.

# 14.

# THE OUTFIELD

## Playing the Outfield

GENE WOODLING

## Fielding Ground Balls

DUKE SNIDER

## Catching in the Outfield

HANK BAUER

## Handling Line Drives

DON MUELLER

## Throwing from the Outfield

CARL FURILLO

# Playing the Outfield

## GENE WOODLING

### New York Yankees

The most important qualifications of an outfielder are speed of foot, the ability to judge fly balls and to have a good throwing arm.

A player who fills all of these demands in championship style is Gene Woodling, great outfielder for the New York Yankees, who here shows the outfielder's "ready" stance. It can be seen that Woodling is so well balanced on both feet he can break into immediate action in almost any direction, thus getting the "jump" on the ball.

Generally speaking, as far as outfield positions are concerned, the player in center field should be the best and fastest fielder in the outfield for it is the center fielder who ordinarily must cover the most territory. It follows, then, that the left fielder should be the second best fielder as most batters are right-handed, resulting in the majority of balls being pulled into left field. Yet, of all three outfielders, the right fielder should have the strongest throwing arm of the lot because he so often must make the long throw to third base.

Probably the most important duty that a young outfielder must master, after learning the difficult feat of how to judge fly balls, is the art of going back for a ball hit over his head. This only comes with practice but the fielder will learn that he can maintain his balance better if he occasionally takes a quick look in front of him while, of course, devoting most of his attention to the flight of the ball.

There also must be close cooperation between the outfielders to avoid injurious collisions when pursuing a fly ball. The first man to call for the catch must be given preference by another outfielder running toward the same spot, but the call should be made repeatedly and loudly. If two outfielders are "camped" under the ball and a decisive throw must be made to the infield, the man with the strongest arm should be allowed to make the catch, in which case the outfielder backing off should advise his teammate to "take it" and then call where the throw should be made.

Outfielders also should be given preference over infielders in taking short fly balls when there are men on base because the infielder is perforce running awkwardly as he twists and turns to see the ball while the outfielder is coming in and, after making the catch, is in better position to let go with a throw.

Another important duty of outfielders is to back up the bases on balls thrown or hit to the infielders. This is done by running to a spot behind but in line with the flight of the ball.

The left fielder should back up second base on throws from the first or second baseman or the right fielder, and back up third base on throws from near the plate or from the first baseman. The center fielder must back up second base to guard against overthrows when the throw is by the pitcher, catcher, first baseman or third baseman. The right fielder backs up first base on throws from near the plate and from third base, as well as on throws from the left fielder along the foul line.

The outfielders also come in immediately during a rundown, backing up the infielders in case of an overthrow.

# Fielding Ground Balls

## DUKE SNIDER
**Brooklyn Dodgers**

Ability to field ground balls is just as necessary for an outfielder as it is for an infielder, because a ground ball in the outfield is a base hit and a momentary bobble is all that is necessary to give an alert base runner an extra base. One of the best fielders in the big leagues, as well as one of the finest hitters, is Duke Snider of the Brooklyn Dodgers who shows how to block a hard rolling smash so it won't get through.

On the normal grounder, which has lost all its steam as it nears the outfielder, it is unnecessary to field the ball in this manner, particularly when it may be more vital to get off a quick throw. In such a case, the outfielder doesn't get down on one knee but scoops up the ball with both hands merely by using a deep body bend with the knees slightly bent.

In the case of ground balls to the outfield, the catch is made with the fingers pointing down and, on bouncing balls, the catch is timed by the charging outfielder so the ball will be taken at the top of its hop.

The outfielder, of course, always gets the ball back to the infield as quickly as possible but the block should be used on all hard-hit balls. The slower method is taken here because a ball hit in this manner is good for a single but, if the ball isn't surely stopped, the runner probably would get an extra base.

In the category of ground balls come the line-drives which there is a chance to catch. An all-out attempt for the shoestring catch is necessary only when the runs which might score could lose the game. In cases where your team has a good lead, or where there are no players in scoring position, the best method is simply to make certain that the ball is blocked and stopped. There is no sense in taking unnecessary chances which might cause physical injury unless it is absolutely necessary in a vital stage of the game.

# Catching in the Outfield

## HANK BAUER

**New York Yankees**

The correct method of taking a high drive in the outfield is demonstrated by Hank Bauer, one of the aces of the New York Yankees. Note that the arms are extended with the thumbs together. Then, as the ball starts to settle into the glove, the hands are drawn back with the ball, easing it out of its flight. If the ball has been hit especially high and its fall is almost straight downward, some outfielders like to take the ball with the heels of the palms together to prevent obstruction of view by the hands.

Most outfielders try to get to where they judge the ball will fall as quickly as possible. This permits them to "camp under it" and be in better position to shift quickly should the flight of the ball be affected by its spin or wind currents.

On some occasions, however, it is better to time the approach so the outfielder will arrive at the right spot just as the ball descends. One such occasion is when the ball is hit into the sun. Playing it for arrival just at the moment when it comes down will permit the outfielder to keep it in view all the time without having the sun in his eyes.

All outfielders should, of course, learn to play the sun field—normally right field and center field because of the manner in which most parks are laid out. Even if you are not in the sun field in your home park, you may play in a rival park where the sun would be in your eyes.

When playing the sun field, it is necessary for the outfielders to wear sunglasses. The type used most widely in the major leagues consists of a pair of glasses on a band which fits around the head. When not needed, the glasses lay up against the underside of the peak of the cap. When a ball is hit into the sun, the glasses are dropped down over the eyes by a quick tap against the outside of the peak of the cap. The glasses are brought into use immediately when the ball is hit near the sun, as the runner starts toward the ball, and not after he has started his pursuit.

Catching fly balls in the outfield, of course, calls for accentuating two points already made.

The first is that much practice is required to go back for balls which are hit over the outfielder's head.

The second is that the first outfielder to call for the ball must be given preference so injurious collisions are avoided, the other outfielder involved circling to the rear of the play to back up the player making he catch.

# Handling Line Drives

## DON MUELLER

**New York Giants**

One of the toughest chores an outfielder must be able to perform is handling line-drives, and the ability to play them correctly often means the difference between victory and defeat. Don Mueller of the New York Giants shows here the quick shift to a throwing position after taking one of those low liners which are so hard to handle.

An attempt at a shoestring catch frequently is necessary if the outcome of the game hangs in the balance. When the winning or tying runs are in position to score, an all-out attempt is necessary. Sometimes a diving catch must be made. In these cases, it must be emphasized, the body should be as relaxed as possible to avoid injury, the dive being made in a flat slide with the arms extended to the front or by doubling up and rolling after the catch is made.

This type of catch only should be employed, however, when absolutely necessary and, if the ball is missed, the outfielder attempts to block the ball with his body so it will not roll too far away.

Remember, though, if the catch is not absolutely vital, it is much better simply to block the ball and make certain that it is stopped.

Most line-drives along the foul lines will curve out into foul territory. Thus, if there are less than two out and there are runners in scoring position, it is better to let the ball drop foul than to make a running catch at the end of which you will not be in a position to make a throw.

The outfielder also must be prepared to handle rebounds off the walls in the outfield. The best method to "learn" the walls is to watch how balls bounce off them in batting practice, for most walls will vary in the distance of the rebound and the angles. Having determined the angle and distance expected in a rebound, the outfielder takes a position facing the wall and then, after scooping up the ball, whirls in the direction of the glove hand to make the throw.

These rebounds often are misjudged due to the varying speed or spin of the ball. That is why the nearest outfielder to the one playing the rebound should back up the play and be in a strategic position to take the ball should it carom in a different direction than the one anticipated.

# Throwing from the Outfield

## CARL FURILLO

**Brooklyn Dodgers**

To be good, a throw from the outfield must be made quickly, accurately and to the right base. Naturally, a strong arm is necessary. Certainly one of the best in the baseball business belongs to iron-armed Carl Furillo, of the Brooklyn Dodgers, who here shows the overhand throw which has cut down countless brash base runners.

Nobody can teach you how to throw a baseball hard, but you can develop accuracy —and a certain amount of arm strength— through practice.

"As for throwing the ball to the proper base," says Furillo, "that comes only with experience and discipline and concentration on what is going on at all times. It probably is the toughest part of the throwing assignment that a young outfielder must master. The best way to do the job right is to know what to do before the play comes up—to go over the possible plays in your mind before, not after, the batter hits the ball."

Concerning the throw itself, it should be low and fast. The ball usually is thrown after a quick hop to provide more momentum to the throw. If the throw is to first or second from right field, the throw is made on the fly because the distance is not too great.

However, on throws to third or home plate from right field, the ball is aimed to come in on the bounce. If you attempt to throw it all the way in the air, the ball must be given so much height that it delays its arrival at the plate. Also, throwing the ball low allows it to be taken by the cutoff man standing between the outfielder and the base to which he is throwing. The cutoff man is the target, giving an accurate line for the throw. Then, if the runner is going to be easily safe, or if another runner tries to advance on the throw, the cutoff man can take the ball and change the direction of the play.

Cutoff men usually play about 40 to 50 feet in front of the base at which the play is to be made and in line with the flight of the ball. The first baseman is the cutoff man on throws to the plate except in the case of singles to left field, when the third baseman is the cutoff man. The shortstop is the cutoff man on throws to second base from left field or left center field, while the second baseman is the cutoff man on throws to second base from right field and right center field.

The closest outfielder to the one making the throw usually calls where the throw should go, having time to size up the situation, but if, like Furillo, you have all the possibilities figured out in advance, you will be that much better prepared to make the correct throw.

Every couple of innings during a game, Furillo advises, the throwing arm should be warmed up by tossing the ball back and forth with another outfielder while the pitcher is warming up. The outfielder may not have had to make any throws for several innings. This prevents the arm from tightening up, particularly in chilly weather.

Just like any other player, the outfielder must take good care of his throwing arm. During spring training it should be worked into shape with as much care as is taken by a pitcher and during the ball season it has to be given enough work to keep it fit.